Special thanks to CJ Wood's "Leo" the Chinese water dragon, & George Godfrey's "Ziggy" the iguana.

Facebook:
https://www.facebook.com/KayjoDesigns

I0116437

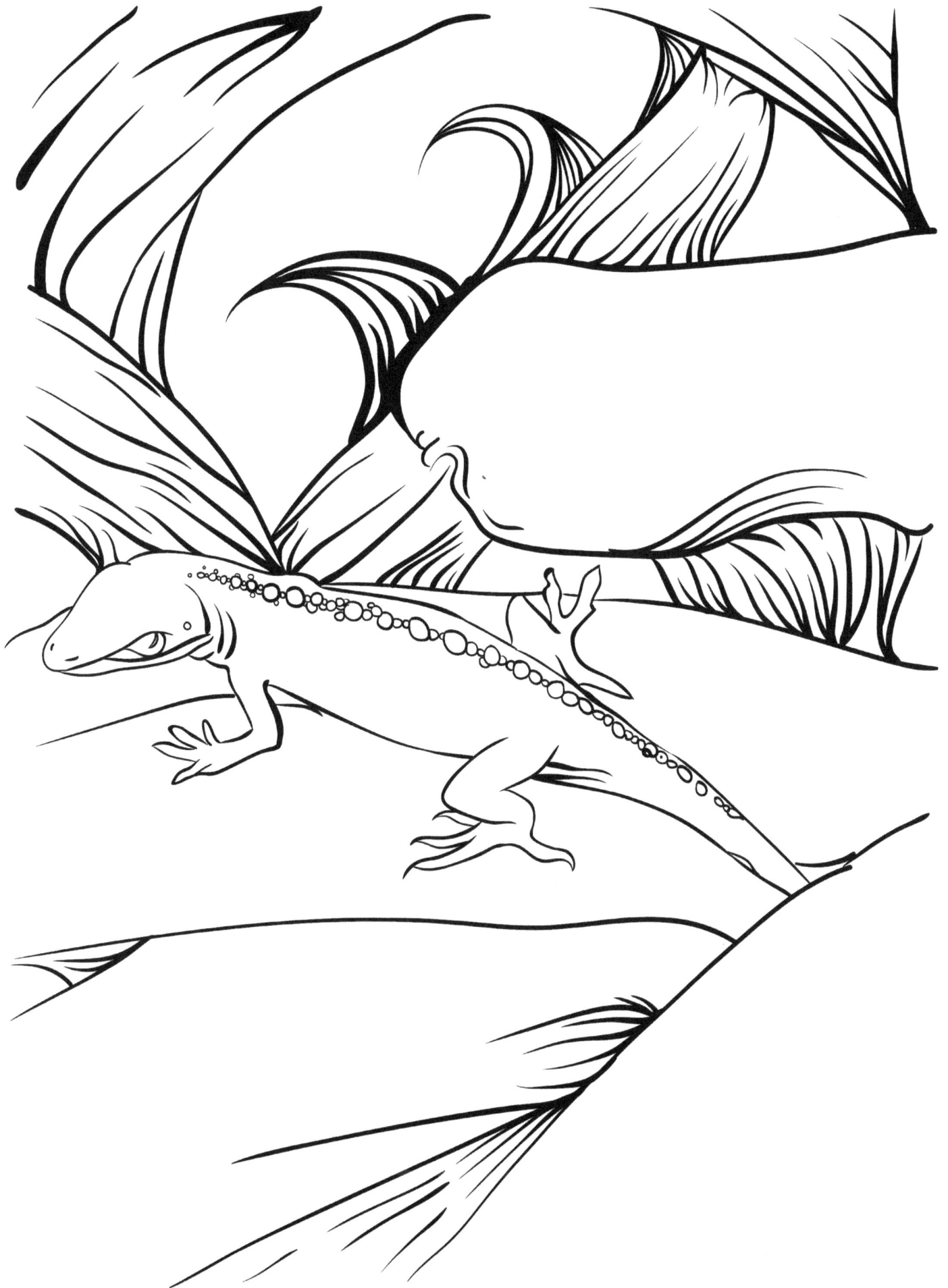

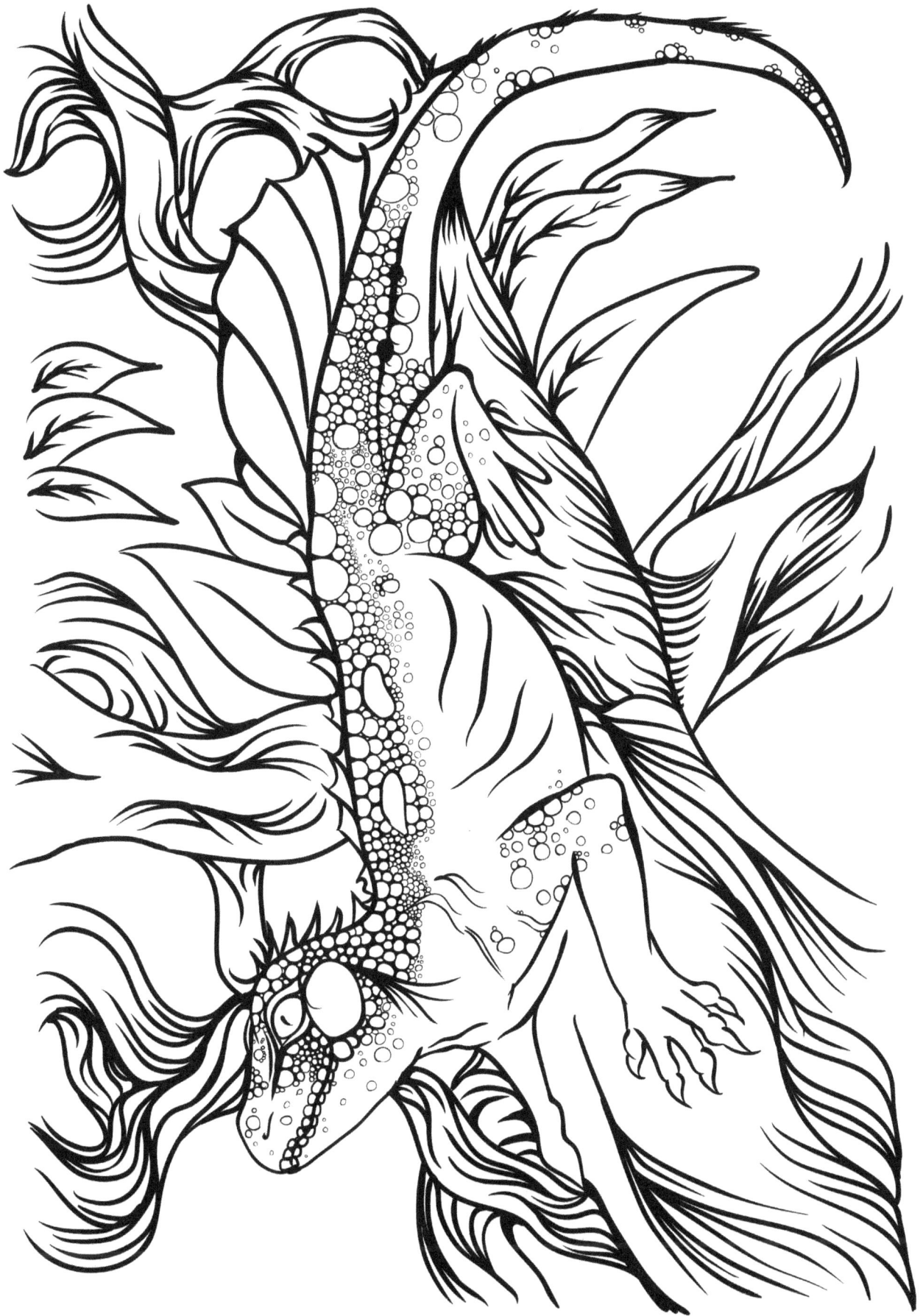

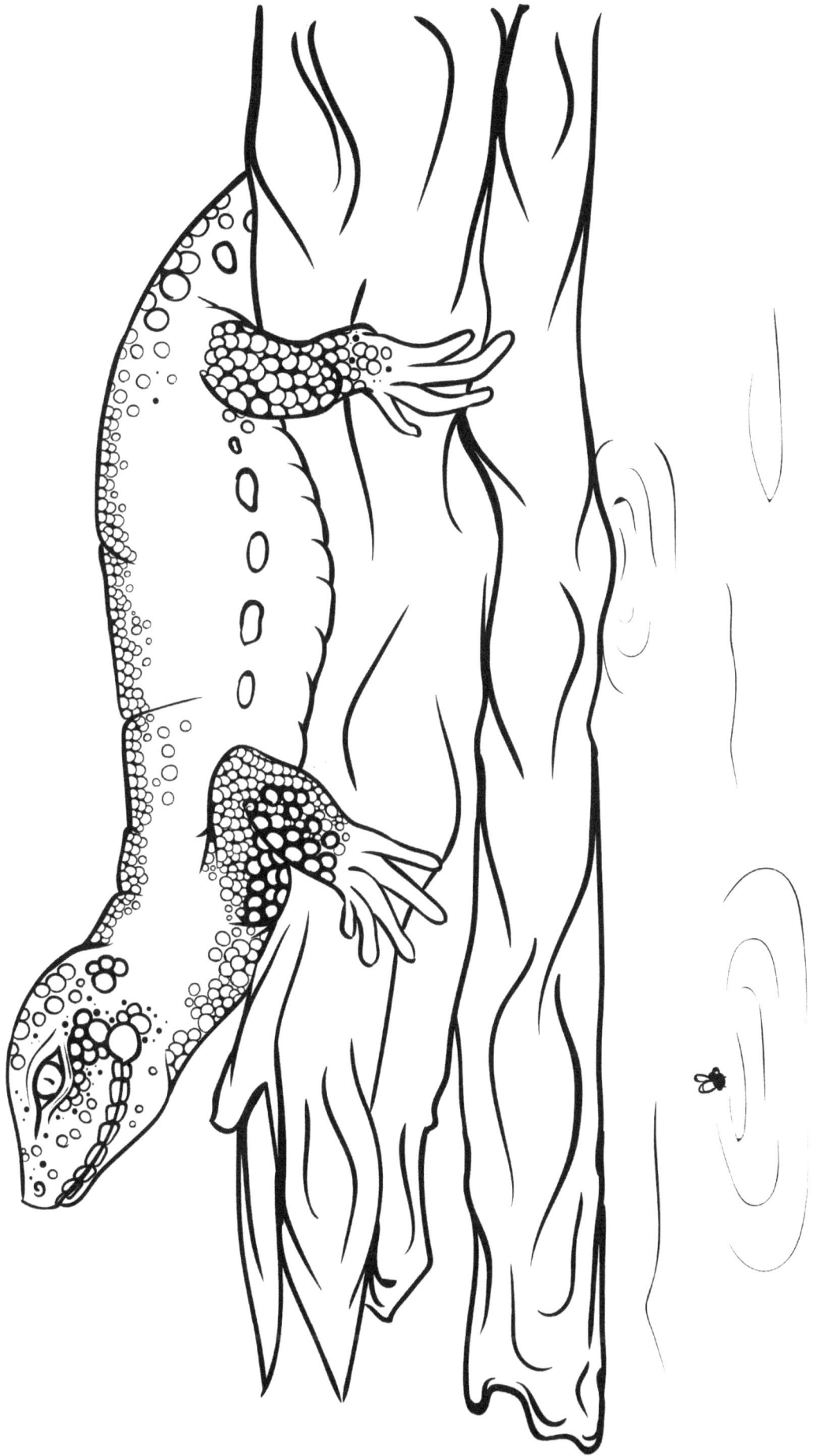

www.ingramcontent.com/pod-product-compliance
Lightning Source LLC
Chambersburg PA
CBHW081721270326
41933CB00017B/3247